Dream
even bigger than what
you are right now and
have faith that your
successes will
be a reality one day.

Simply Badd

Succeeding

When Others Don't Want You To

2021 And Beyond

Winning - At All Cost

by T-Ronn Hicks aka

Simply Badd

2nd paperback edition Oct 2022

Book design by TRonn Hicks and Kafi Ahmad

ISBN 979-8-9851987-6-8

Shuga Shuga Publishing LLC
ssbookpllc@gmail.com
(214)727-4496

Table of Contents

Dedication

This book is dedicated to my Lord and Savior, Jesus Christ. Without Him, there is no T-Ronn Hicks. I would also like to dedicate this to my incredible family — my phenomenal wife Marian, daughter Lexi, son Zayy, and all my sisters and brothers, aunts, uncles, cousins, extended family from all over, and of course, our family dog Rolf!

I would also like to dedicate this book to the Lewisville ISD students, parents, administrators, and the Parent-Teacher Association communities worldwide. Finally, this book is dedicated to all the awesome people who are tired of being ordinary and are seriously ready to become extraordinary! This is for you...

SUCCEEDING: When Others
Don't Want You To

You must go through something to become something GREAT!

T-Ronn Hicks aka

Simply Badd

Foreword

All of us aspire to be great. We've laid in bed late at night and drifted off to sleep thinking of achieving big things — maybe it was to be a famous actor, someone who ends up doing extraordinary things for other people. Perhaps it was a transcendent athlete, skill levels likened to Michael Jordan, Serena Williams, or Tom Brady. We all have huge dreams and unquenchable desires for greatness. For the most part, there are always supportive people around us who challenge us to make those dreams a reality. Now imagine if you repeatedly heard, "You'll never make it" or "You might as well give up on that dream right now kid!"

Your first thought is to ignore the haters and keep 'doing you'. But once something like that is said and put out there in the atmosphere, it is painfully difficult to let it go — especially if those words came from the mouth of someone close to you. Hard to say, "Ah — who cares what that person thinks!" You look to them for positive reinforcement, affirmation, and to be a voice of reason. You lean on them for support so it's hurtful when you end up getting the opposite reaction.

News flash!

THEY ARE NOT YOU!

And I am here to share with you that if you can dream it and believe it, then you should open your arms and RECEIVE it! Granted, you're probably thinking that having such a positive attitude is easier said than done. But it's not. I can say that because I've been there. From as early as the young age of 6 years old, I was bullied relentlessly. Kids picked on me for everything, whether it was my height, weight, the way I walked or spoke, or even my inability to spell words correctly. I was told that I wasn't good enough, and it would have been easy for me to believe that. Instead, I carved my own path — always believing that I was meant to do something big. And you know what? I was right. I became a professional wrestler and parlayed that into ongoing humanitarian efforts geared toward lifting other people. I wrote a book. In fact, I have written several books. I became a community leader, husband, father, and confidante to so many people. I became a business owner, leader, and the owner of a Kentucky Derby champion horse — all because I believe in ME!

If you're still with me, then you're already walking down the right path. All I ask is that you block out the noise, continue to read this book, and maybe think about sharing it with others who have similar goals of becoming extraordinary.

I believe in you.

Do you?

Chapter 1
I Can & I Will

I have dreamed big ever since I can remember. When others told me that I couldn't do something, I remained focus on what I knew could become a reality. My motto has always been, "Tell me that I can't, and I'll show you that I can — and will!" I think I've even said it verbatim to a few non-believers over the years. While they may have scoffed at the time, I was always able to prove them wrong.

Granted, my ability to succeed has not come easy. There's a lot of hard work involved. Even today, I struggle with procrastination, time management issues, and distractions that for some people, may only sidetrack them for a few hours but can knock me off the rail for days on end.

One thing I have never struggled with is excuses. I simply don't believe in them. I've also never wavered in my faith — my faith in God and my faith in ME.

I'll level with you, the reason why I have succeeded so much in life isn't because of dumb luck, chance, coincidence, or four or five rich friends giving me handouts. My success is because of my faith. You're probably saying to yourself, "Man there is no way everything you've done can be pointed directly back to faith." But I promise you, it's true! And here is proof. When I was 7 years old, I was ready to quit life. I mean it. I was D.O.N.E. I mentioned earlier that I was relentlessly bullied for the majority of my childhood, and I had reached a point where it seemed like everything was crashing down on me all at once. But just when I was about to quit, something magical happened. I fell in love with the sport of professional wrestling. I had two friends at the time, Herb Davis and Bill Breckenridge. Herb's dad was the one who took us to my very first live event. Bill and I didn't miss a single one after that. As I told the Cross Timbers Gazette in November 2020, I was hooked by the theatrically animated battle between good and evil, larger-than-life characters you can't help but cheer for, and all those death-defying leaps off the top rope. I genuinely believed I could don a pair of wrestling tights one day and even become a world champion. All I needed was the right push.

Well, as FAITH would have it, I met my favorite wrestler, the late Rocky Soulman Johnson, one Tuesday night at the Louisville Gardens. If you don't know who Rocky Soulman Johnson was, you missed out. His list of accolades is too long to include in this book, but if you need a hint, he was Dwayne The Rock Johnson's dad! I remember being ridiculously nervous to meet him, but I was also incredibly excited and wasn't about to waste this opportunity. So, I asked him, "what is the key to a successful life?"

He told me, "Write down your dreams and goals on an index card or piece of paper and look at them daily. The more you see them, the more they become you." Well, that night, I went home and wrote down my goals.

1. Stop being bullied by the time I reached 13 years old.

2. Become a successful professional wrestler.

3. Stop bullying worldwide.

I looked at that list every day and just like Rocky said, I began to believe that not only could I accomplish these lofty goals, but I could accomplish anything.

1. No one bullied me ever again by the age of 12.

2. I wrestled under the name of Simply Badd for 18 years and won 19 world titles on the independent circuit, becoming a five-time Hall of Famer.

3.   Eradicating bullying worldwide is a quest I'm still on today. My Simply Badd Ministry and outreach and mentoring programs such as Stop Bullying Our Purpose (S.B.O.P.) are all geared toward that anti-bullying message and building stronger, loving, and caring communities one child at a time.

Trust me when I say that none of this is by coincidence, and it certainly wasn't because of my good looks. I'm a witness, good things happen because of faith. I have been called "The Brother of Faith" because, despite everything I've been through, I made my dreams happen.

So, I urge you to continue to dream big. Dream even bigger than what you are dreaming right now and have faith that your successes will be a reality one day.

Remember:

"Write down your dreams and goals on an index card or piece of paper and look at them daily. The more you see them, the more they become you."

— Rocky 'Soulman' Johnson

Chapter 2
Let's Face These Challenges

In life, you will face challenges. Most people hear "challenges" and immediately leap to negative thinking. And who can blame you? But having said that, we could all stand to re-train our brains to think about challenges in a more positive light.

After all, if it weren't for daily challenges, what could push us to that next level? Challenges aren't meant to hurt you. Yes, they are tough. And one challenge after the other can seem like someone on a higher level wants to see you fail. But that couldn't be further from the truth. Challenges give us all the courage to bring that inner person — the one who will succeed no matter what adversity they come across — to real life.

To illustrate my point, imagine eating a chocolate cake without chocolate in it. You probably can't imagine it because that's not possible. A chocolate cake that doesn't have chocolate in it simply can't be a chocolate cake. Right? Right! Well, the same can be said about life. A life without challenges isn't life.

I know that's a super weird analogy, but the more and more you think about it, you have to admit that it makes a lot of sense. All I'm saying is that you have to ask yourself, "How much better am I now that I have survived that challenge?"

Furthermore, ask yourself, "How much more prepared am I to handle whatever challenge happens next simply because I survived the previous challenge?"

My life was made better because of the challenges I faced growing up. I know that now — despite all the bullying, the self-doubt, and all the times I just wanted to throw my hands up and quit. My life is better because I'm stronger now. Yes, I got stronger physically because I worked out in the gym. But more importantly, I became stronger mentally and emotionally because of the challenges I faced and conquered.

A quick side note: To be successful in life, you can't stay stuck in park and neutral. Those are two of your worst friends (park and neutral). And on top of that, you can't go switch to reverse, either. That's your third-worst enemy — and if you do that, you'll always be stuck living in your past problems. You'll never become the person The Lord meant for you to become, and you won't live the fulfilled life that you were placed on this earth to live out.

Instead, you must always be in drive and have a full-throttle mindset if you want to succeed.

Another saying that I've lived by for years: "You must go through something to become something great!' For example, Steve Harvey has continually shared the story of how he was homeless for three years. He lived inside his car and lost everything he ever possessed. He was at his wit's end, but he faced his challenges like a true hero. And then, one day, he got the call to come to the Apollo Theater in Harlem.

Eric Thomas, America's top motivational speaker, has also shared stories about his journey as a homeless man. At the time, his girlfriend told him that if he was going to be in her life, he had to get a diploma. She was going to college, so there was no excuse for him not to go, too. She challenged him to get a GED and follow her to college — and he did.

Les Brown, another speaker, was told he was academically challenged.

Joel Osteen was sued by the largest taxpayer in Texas to prevent him from moving into his church, but he survived that challenge, and he now has that church. You know it as

Lakewood Church in Houston, Texas.

I share these examples with you to help you see that it's important to go through challenges to reach the next level in life. The second that you start second-guessing yourself is when you need to take a look back at this chapter and remind yourself of all the great people who managed to find a way through the darkest points of their lives.

If they can do it, so can you! Let's face these challenges head-on.

Chapter 3
See The Vision

A strategy that has always helped me achieve my goals is to write them down on a piece of paper or index card. I mentioned this in Chapter 1, and, frankly, it cannot be overstated.

There is something permanent about writing your goals down. You're making a commitment to yourself; however informal the process may seem at first. Honestly, it's pretty powerful stuff. Writing it all down and displaying it prominently somewhere (on your bathroom mirror, on a corkboard in your bedroom, or even on the front of the refrigerator) means you're more likely to be reminded of those promises every day.

You see it, commit it to memory, and seek out ways to achieve it. Furthermore, you're more likely to ask yourself, "What have I done today to take at least one positive step toward achieving my hopes and dreams?"

My intention with this chapter is not to get too long-winded. The basic message is to simply remind you that if you want to succeed in life, write your goals down. Get up off the couch, drive to Walmart, Target, or your favorite store, walk over to the school supply section, and grab the following items:

- **Ruler**
- **Glue stick**
- **Scissors**
- **Posterboard**
- **Magazines**

With these items, you will create what many refer to as a "Vision Board!"

I began using vision boards in 2010. This is a bountiful blessing, one unique key to my success that I have been able to enjoy for years and years.

As Rocky said to me all those years ago, "In order to enjoy your vision, you must see your vision daily." I took those words to heart, and you should also.

If you desire to be all you can be in life, you must be serious about success, have the willingness to work harder than everyone else, have the grit to constantly be in overdrive, and be willing to always have your goals on display so that they are always on your mind. Remember, this is your vision. This is your dream, your desire, your goal, your ambition. No one will do it for you. It is up to you. Now do it!

The next several chapters are meant to be quick-hitter tips and tricks that anyone who wants to succeed in life must adhere to.

Chapter 4
Stop Procrastinating

Sometimes, we just need to get out of our own way and stop sabotaging ourselves. We like to think that there are a ton of external obstacles holding us back in life, but the harsh reality is that the biggest obstacle is ourselves! Nine times out of 10, it's because we are constantly procrastinating.

For example, have you ever told yourself the following ...

"Oh, I can do that tomorrow."

"That class assignment isn't due for another week, I've got time."

"It can wait a few more hours."

"I just don't want to right now."

Sure, you have. We all have. Even myself. I'm notorious for being a massive procrastinator. It's one of my deepest regrets in life. Because what happens is that instead of following through with what we promised that we would do, we put it off. Then, we put it off some more. Then again and again and again. Like punching the snooze button on the alarm clock, we're delaying what we should be doing — setting ourselves back. And for what — a chance to sit on the couch?

When this happens, your procrastination not only hurts you but also affects those close to you. It's all one giant circle. It's up to us to break it.

Remember that we are called to leave a legacy for our children's children. Do you want that legacy to be procrastination? Is that what you want people to remember you by?

Do you want your children and their children to follow in those same footsteps? You can't be successful if you keep putting things off and making excuses not to become successful.

Push yourself to always keep the pedal to the metal. Remind yourself that this is the time to focus! Focus your life and release the greatness that lies inside of you.

Chapter 5
Be Hungry, Stay Hungry

I've always tried my best to make a difference in the communities I serve. One thing I noticed our communities need more of is "inspiration". Yes, we've gone through plenty of "storms" over the past year between the COVID-19 pandemic, racial injustices, political battles that have seemingly put everyone at odds, but it's our choice to stay embroiled in those storms or lift ourselves out of the weeds, inject some positivity and hunger back into our lives, and keep moving forward. I say Let's roll people! Let's find our hunger again.

For me to get better in life, I must work on myself daily, weekly, monthly, and yearly to become the best ME possible — both for myself and everyone I come into contact with. I remind myself every day that "I'm getting better for myself," not because of what others think or say about me. Because at the end of the day, if I'm not intentionally changing my life for the best, I will never become the man my family needs me to be.

I'm not alone in this belief. Here are just a few inspiring words from people who have walked the walk and talked the talk.

"Many of us never realize our greatness because we get sidetracked by secondary activities. We spread ourselves so thin that we cannot stay focused on set goals and dreams to achieve greatness."

— The University of Success by Og Mandino

"You have to have that DAWG mindset to win at life." — Eric Thomas

I particularly love the quote from Mr. Thomas. For those who don't know, "DAWG" is an urban street term that means "total grit." It's the determination to let no one, let nothing stop you from becoming great! I've tried my best to incorporate that mindset into how I live my life.

When I got serious about my life, began tasting success, overcoming obstacles, and refusing to listen to negative talk from others; it was then that I began making a difference in myself, my life, and the lives around me.

Chapter 6
Having a Millionaire Mindset

When most of us think about millionaires, our mind gravitates to ridiculously wealthy individuals who have seven or eight sports cars, a mansion in the hills, and the ability to spend money on whatever they want at a moment's notice. When I hear the word millionaire, I think 'MINDSET'

To be a millionaire, you have to see yourself as one — before you have the money to back up the claim. In Chapter 3, I spoke on having a vision and acting on it to achieve the success you want and deserve.

This is an absolute must-have if you want to be a millionaire. People have put that mindset into practice all their life and you can too. It's your mind. Set the mind and the mind is set…MINDSET

Michael Jordan saw himself as a winner long before he was winning.

Dwayne The Rock Johnson saw himself as a very charismatic leader — both in professional wrestling and as a movie star — long before it became a reality.

Ric Flair, perhaps the greatest wrestler of all time (sorry Rock), saw himself as a "limousine riding, jet flying son of a gun" before everyone else did.

Those are just three examples. There are many more, whether it be Kobe Bryant, Steve Harvey, Serena Williams, or someone else. And they all say the same thing: "Victory Starts In The Mind — And Then Your Wallet And Bank Account Will Follow!"

Having a millionaire mindset is not a normal way of thinking. But it is certainly what leads you down the path of making the right changes in your life so that you can reach the goals you've always wanted. It requires that you OWN IT. You must be ready to refocus your mind and change how you think about yourself, your finances, and the world around you.

Chapter 7

Create a Winning Action Plan

Remember these golden rules about dreams:

A dream that's written down with a date becomes a goal.

A goal broken down into steps becomes a plan.

A plan backed by action makes your dreams become reality!

Success is predictable when it is based on hard work and your willingness to succeed. As I always say, "I can't cheat the grind. It knows how much I have invested. It will not give me anything I haven't worked for!"

A pencil and paper or constant notes inside your phone have to become your best friend. That is, of course, if you are truly serious about being successful.

The Warren Buffets, Mark Cubans, Grant Cardones, Tom Bradys, Steph Currys, and the LeBron Jameses of the world already have the next day planned in their planners — whether it's a paper planner or in their phones.

The successful people I named above are out of bed by 3 a.m. to start their day.

Warren Buffet and Mark Cuban are watching financial reports on the news.

LeBron and Steph are in the gym working out and mastering their crafts.

You may say they are crazy and yes, I agree. But crazy people are successful people! A winning action plan consists of dreams, goals, and hard work. Granted, some of us will have to work harder than others. But it's worth it!

For years, I told my beautiful wife, Marian, that we would own a Kentucky Derby champion. And on September 5, 2020, it became a reality. I may not own the entire horse, but through a partnership, I do. I believe that I'm the first professional wrestler to own a Kentucky Derby champion! The naysayers may say that all I did was invest. They're right, but that doesn't change the fact that I had to follow all the steps that I shared above.

Ask yourself these two questions:

How bad do I want to be successful?

What am I willing to do to make this happen?

Once you have the answers to those two questions, it's time to ACT.

Let's make it happen! I believe in you!

Chapter 8

It's "Let's Go" Time

In 2002, superstar rapper Eminem released a song called, "Lose Yourself."

I'm not a huge rap fan, but I do love music with a message, and this song is one of my favorites because it speaks the truth. It's also very inspiring.

This may not be exact, but here is a small sampling of the lyrics:

Look, if you only had one shot, one opportunity to seize everything you ever wanted in one moment, would you capture it, or would you just let it slip!?

You better lose yourself in the music, the moment you own it, you better never let it go. You only get one shot, don't miss your chance to blow. This opportunity comes once in a lifetime.

Once I listened to this song a few times, I knew it was speaking to me. It was like Eminem was telling me to become a better person both inside and out.

The phrase that's used a lot among teams is, " Let's Go," to get fired up before a game or event. The professional football player that coined that phrase during his career was Dallas Cowboy Legend, Emmitt Smith. Emmitt has always had a way with words, just like Eminem. He has been quoted as saying, "Super Bowls are won in the offseason!"

Most people may not know this, but Emmitt Smith began working out again the day after winning Super

Bowl XXVII. He had just climbed the mountaintop with his teammates and was already determined to win Super Bowl XXVIII.

And They Did!

I share this with you because winning at anything — life, professional football, professional wrestling, or even at being one of the world's top rappers — you must first step outside the box and do the things that others wouldn't normally do.

The difference between ordinary and extraordinary is extra!

You must be willing to do extra to be different than the ordinary.

Extraordinary people aren't in a box. They are in a circle!

Chapter 9
Be a Planted Seed

In life, it's so easy for all of us to get caught up listening to other people. We trust their thoughts, especially those who are close to us such as family and close friends. But really, doing so puts us inside a box.

So, if I am in a box, I can't possibly grow — mentally or physically.

Once I stop listening and being contaminated by other's opinions — no matter how kind-hearted those opinions may have been — I decided to stop living in a box and start living my life inside a circle. In a box, I am not allowed to grow because I'm being contained based on others' negative thoughts about me or my decisions. In a circle, my seed that's placed inside the right soil will grow from being watered and taken care of.

There are no limits.

I am growing because my roots can spread, all with the positivity from those watering me with the right resources. I need to continually pour greatness into my life so that I can become that winner that I am meant to be.

To grow, I must let go of the excuses!

Chapter 10
No More Excuses

The definition of an excuse is to release yourself from duty and responsibility, or an attempt to lessen the blame attached to a fault or offense.

As we can see in everyday life, it's easy to have an excuse. Excuses are all around us. Perhaps we didn't complete our goals, plans, task, or honey-do lists, so we create excuses rather than owning up to our own shortcomings.

If you can't tell already, I cannot stand excuses. I don't make them, and I really have to shake my head at people who do. Excuses are like walking around all day with crutches when you really don't need them. It's just a cop-out for not walking normally, and I have learned the more excuses that a person makes, the less likely they are to achieve and accomplish what they want in life.

Excuses place limits on our vision. And when this happens, the less we will succeed in life — period. End of story.

Chapter 11
How Bad Do I Want It?

Legendary rapper Tupac had a song called, "How Do You Want It, How Do Ya Feel!" I wrote earlier about Eminem's incredibly inspiring lyrics, but Tupac's lyrics are a little more eye-opening.

My spin on the lyrics of this world class rapper says, "How bad do you want it, how bad do you feel, coming up fast in the cash game for real."

In life, we all want to have success fast. But at what cost? I'm willing to work hard and secure my legacy because I want to honor all that my mother, my single mother did and how it made me the man that I am today. I watched her work three jobs to raise five kids. She never quit. She

never made excuses. She never
stopped. She simply worked hard.
She showed us how bad she wanted
it for us.

**There must be a hunger
inside of me so I can
prove how bad I want it.**

Chapter 12

Make Your Hand a
Winning One

I look at life as a card game — card games like Go Fish, Spades, Speed, Or High Stakes Poker. Sometimes in life, you have to play the hand that's dealt. It's just the way it is. Well, I don't know if that is entirely true. I had a conversation recently with a nice lady named Holly Plunkett, and we both agreed that while cards are a game of chance, in the game of life, it's up to you to make the hand you are dealt a winning hand.

Sure life isn't fair, it never will be, but too many people hyper focus on what's fair or what's not fair. They are always playing the "shoulda-coulda-woulda" game.

"If I woulda done this, I coulda done that."

"If the game were fairer, I coulda done this."

Well, my response to that mindset is this: the longer you play that game, the longer it will take you to become successful.

A perfect example is my own life. I know from years of experience that I have continually been the victim of racism. It's not fair. It's unjust. I do not deserve it, and neither do my family or anyone else I know. But you know what? I don't focus on any of that. Because I refuse to play into a game of *Distraction Reaction*.

Distraction Reaction is when others see that you have an agenda, and you are focused on it. They think, "Well, if I can cause a distraction of some type, then I can definitely get a negative reaction from this person." In turn, you'll lose focus on your purpose and agenda. This sort of game plays out daily in boardrooms, courtrooms, on the streets you walk on every day, and sometimes in bedrooms. Yes, there is something to be said about "playing the hand that you are dealt." Instead of settling for the hand that you've been dealt, play it!

It's the only way to win in this game called life.

I want to honor what my
mother, a
single parent mom did,
and how it made me the
man that I am today. I
watched
her work three jobs to
raise five kids. She never
quit. She never made
excuses. She never
stopped. She worked
hard. She showed us
how bad she was

Simply Badd

Chapter 13
Network With Winners

I have learned countless lessons throughout my life.

One is to "never ask a broke person how to get rich."

I have many other lessons. Some are offensive, so they will not be in this book. But others are great lessons to live by. If you desire to be successful financially, you must begin to network with those who have reached financial success.

You cannot ask people to give advice on subjects they have yet to master.

I have several friends that are millionaires. As a result, their day is different than mine. For example, at

4 a.m., I'm doing my morning devotional. By 5 a.m., I'm headed to the gym. By 6:30 a.m., I'm home and taking a shower so that by 7:50 a.m., I've already dropped the kids off at school. But wait, there's more.

By 9 a.m., I'm busy with Life Coaching. I do that for most of the day until 2:30 p.m., and then it's back to the gym again (helps keep my stress level to a minimum, and my family will not let me come home stressed out). Between 4:30 p.m. and 8:30 p.m., I'm making a slew of business calls. Then I have a few hours to spend with my family before going off to bed by 10:30 p.m.

My friends' schedules are drastically different. At 3 a.m., they are watching CNN financial reports. They do devotionals at 4:30 a.m. like I do and are also at the gym by 5:30 p.m., back home at a similar time to shower and eat. But by 8:15 a.m., they are on the phone with their financial planner because the New York Stock Exchange is open for business.

There are some similarities, but you can see the difference. Regardless of where you fit in that scheduling, these are the steps to get you closer to your destiny.

Their suggestion to me is that I'm going to have to adjusts in my lifestyle to live the life I choose to live.

You must be willing to
become a
risk-taker!

Simply Badd

Chapter 14
Risk-Takers Win

As a life coach who has the pleasure of working with high school athletes in Lewisville, TX, I encourage them to take risks. I always tell them that regardless of whether you are on the field or court — play "lights-out."

When you are in the classroom, educate yourself to succeed once you're no longer in the comfortable setting of the classroom or this community.

Furthermore, I believe you only get better when you compete with the best. Competing starts with you taking risks. You must take risks at all costs in order to shut your critics up! Being a risk-taker is a very important part of succeeding when others don't want you to.

Here are some famous risk-takers who succeed in life:

- **Muhammad Ali**
- **Ellen DeGeneres**
- **Steve Harvey**
- **Eric Thomas**
- **T. D. Jakes**
- **Cesar Chavez**
- **Warren Buffett**
- **Les Brown**
- **Amelia Earhart**
- **Frederick Douglas**
- **Bill Gates**
- **Steve Jobs**
- **Nelson Mandela**

And that's just to name a few. My buddy Andy Plunkett once told me, "you can't make it to second if you're always stuck at home!" Could you see your names added to a prominent list of successful risk-takers? All you have to do is "Jump in the fire and go for it!"

Chapter 15
It All Boils Down To You

I have shared some remarkable information on succeeding when others don't want you to by using the 14 tips in the previous chapters, but if you want to become the person you have on your vision board — the person you dream about becoming — it's truly up to you!

There is no mountain you can't climb. There isn't enough criticism that can convince you to give up. No jail cell can hold you from becoming who you are destined to be.

You must become so serious in your actions, shifting the mindset in your subconscious, and see yourself succeeding in all areas of your life;

then, the rest will follow. It is only then that you will reach your destiny.

Regardless of how many haters you have in your life, you must not listen to them or let them get inside your head.

Remember, a critic is a chicken who's second to succeed and does not want others to get there first.

Chapter 16
Words of Wisdom

Whether you believe in God or not, read these Bible scriptures for the next 90 days to help you achieve the level of success that you have in your mind. I challenge you. Watch the shift it creates in your life.

- **Psalm 18:1-3**
- **Isaiah 54:17**
- **I Chronicle 4:9-10**
- **Prov 3:5-6**
- **Luke 2:52**
- **Matt 17:20**
- **Mark 11:23**
- **Mark 11:24**
- **Prov 18:21 (Speak death over the things you don't want in your life. Speak life into things you want in your life)**

Please add your name and your family's name into these scriptures and watch victory and success come into your life!

This is your year. It doesn't matter if we are dealing with COVID-19, a snow-storm, financial downfall, political corruption, racial injustice, haters, naysayers, or something else.

Nothing Can Stop YOU!

It's GO Time!

Let's Go
Succeed
While Others
Don't Want
You To!

Acknowledgments

To the parents, principals, counselors, teachers, and my incredible students, all of whom challenge me to "bring it" daily, stay young at heart, and expect me to be real without sugarcoating reality and facts.

As this book motivates you, turn it into momentum and SUCCEED! I'd like to give a special thanks to Steve Gamel with Edit This, LLC, KK Nyquist, and C Miller at Shuga Shuga Publishing LLC. Thank you for helping me stay organized to make this book a reality.

Finally, thank all of you that believed in yourself enough to invest in yourself and purchase this book. Be blessed

Succeeding

When Others Don't Want You To

2021 And Beyond

Winning - At All Cost

www.ingramcontent.com/pod-product-compliance
Lightning Source LLC
Chambersburg PA
CBHW071017040426
42443CB00007B/821